T0012240

STRONGER THAN YESTERDAY

Published in 2022 by OH!
An Imprint of Welbeck Non-Fiction Limited,
part of Welbeck Publishing Group.
Based in London and Sydney.
www.welbeckpublishing.com

ISBN 978-1-80069-423-1

Compiled and written by: Malcolm Croft

Editorial: Victoria Denne
Project manager: Russell Porter
Design: Tony Seddon
Production: Jess Brisley

A CIP catalogue record for this book is available from the British Library

Printed in China

10 9 8 7 6 5 4 3 2 1

THE LITTLE GUIDE TO

BRITNEY SPEARS

STRONGER THAN YESTERDAY

CONTENTS

INTRODUCTION – 6

08
CHAPTER
ONE

OH, BABY
BABY

50
CHAPTER
TWO

ORIGINAL
DOLL

84
CHAPTER
THREE

FEMME
FATALE

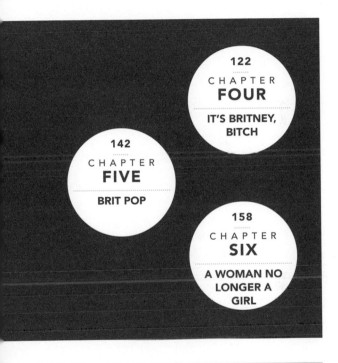

122

CHAPTER
FOUR

IT'S BRITNEY,
BITCH

142

CHAPTER
FIVE

BRIT POP

158

CHAPTER
SIX

A WOMAN NO
LONGER A
GIRL

INTRODUCTION

In 1999, at the age of 17, Britney Jean Spears was effectively crowned the "Princess of Pop" when she dropped her debut single and music video, "Baby One More Time". That song, that video, *that Catholic schoolgirl outfit* ushered in the new millennium and put the whole world in a very good mood. Ever since, our Brit has turned heads and set a billion fingers wagging everywhere she dare adventure – creatively and personally.

Today, the Bible-belt-born-Brit-turned-not-that-innocent-nymph has sold more than 150 million records worldwide, released 48 singles – most of them classic club bangers – and recorded nine studio albums, the culminative success of which has made her not just one of the planet's bestselling popstars of the 21st century, but of all time. She also starred in the movie *Crossroads*, but you'll be forgiven if you've forgotten all about that.

In the second phase of her many comebacks and reinventions, Britney's incredible professional accomplishments – including her range of 34 fragrances, now a multi-billion-dollar franchise – became overwhelmingly overshadowed by her personal life and relationships, particularly since that head-shaving meltdown in 2008, that locked the "emotionally wrecked" singer into a toxic conservatorship led by her father, Jamie Spears. For a while, the world thought that they had lost their favourite femme fatale to yet another celebrity car crash they couldn't look away from.

But this is Britney, bitch. Not only did she take the hits every single time, but she also came back stronger with each one. In 2022, Britney is healthier, happier and freer than ever before. And she's got the incredible abs, the handsome husband, and plans for her next comeback to prove it one…more…time.

This tiny tome is a testament to Britney Spears' true OG status, a snacky celebration of her life-less-ordinary in music, as compact as it is comprehensive. It's action-packed with classic Britney crack-ups, jibes and vibes, insights and hindsight – basically everything us Britaholics need to know, in her words, about why this particular pop princess was born to make us all happy.

Enjoy!

CHAPTER
ONE

OH, BABY BABY

With just five syllables –
oh-ba-by-ba-by – in that sultry Southern
lilt, a legend was born. Britney's first
banger, 'Baby One More Time' was a
tune that set off a worldwide wave of
Britney-mania that no one could resist
and paved the way for Britney to
change popular culture forever.

Britney's first album *Baby One More Time* is one of the best-selling debuts of all time, with more than 25 million copies sold worldwide.

The video to the song of the same name has been viewed on YouTube more than 750 million times, and has over half a billion Spotify streams.

Her career-spanning collection of songs have been streamed more than 3.7 billion times.

66

It's overwhelming! Just
two years ago I was
a completely normal
teenager doing normal
things, and now it's crazy!

99

Britney, on her rise to fame, *TV Hits* magazine,
9 July 1999.

❝

People have said my success is because of just my image, but it's not – I mean, it helps. But even before seeing me, people bought my single. Then, when my video was played, people loved it 'cos it showed a teenager doing something they wanted to do. Teenagers can relate to me and what I'm singing about.

❞

Britney, on her music video to 'Baby One More Time', *TV Hits* magazine, 9 July 1999.

66

My intention was, honestly, seriously, not to be sexy.

99

Britney, on the 'Baby One More Time' video,
The Guardian, 14 September 2008.

"

You just hear it, and you're like, oh my God, if somebody else takes this song, you're gonna kill yourself, you know what I mean?

"

Britney, on knowing what a hit song sounds like, interview by Jenny Eliscu, *Rolling Stone*, 28 November 2011.

66

Sometimes I really do wish
I could just be a singer
and not be famous.

99

Britney, on fame, interview by Jo Elvin,
Glamour magazine, 20 March 2003.

Hollywood heartthrob Ryan Gosling feels responsible for giving Britney her first ever sex advice, back when they were members of the Mickey Mouse Club.

"They [Britney and Christina Aguilera] would come and ask me questions about sex. I just told them what I heard – like positions and stuff. Their mothers went to Disney and told them I was corrupting their kids. I feel somewhat responsible for how sexual she is right now. When I see her with a snake around her neck, I think, *Did I do that?*"

"

If the song calls for me
to wear something a
little voluptuous or sexy,
I like to go there.

"

Britney, on wearing sexy onstage outfits, interview by
Jenny Eliscu, *The Observer*, 16 September 2001

66

Being in the studio a lot, I've been really inspired about beats. You get on the little machine. When you first get on it, you think everything you do sounds good. And I was playing around, and I was feeling it, and I look around and everybody's like, 'Yeah, yeah, yeah, it's good, Britney.' And I started thinking, 'Oh, Britney, this probably sounds like such shit.'

99

Britney, on playing drum machines in the studio, interview by Jenny Eliscu, *The Observer*, 16 September 2001.

It was Britney who came up with the schoolgirl concept for the "Baby One More Time" music video.

"They had this really bizarre video idea to do an animated *Power Ranger*-y thing. I said, 'This is not right.' I had this idea where we're in school and bored out of our minds, and we have Catholic uniforms on. And I said, 'Why don't we have knee-highs and tie the shirts up to give it a little attitude?' – so it wouldn't be boring and cheesy."

"

I've wanted to perform since I was four.

"

Britney, on wanting to perform from a young age,
Sky Customer magazine, 24 November 2000.

"

Five million. Was I tempted? Oh Lord no!

"

Britney, on the American businessman who
offered Britney five million dollars to sleep with him,
FHM magazine, 29 September 2000.

66

You know a girl can walk into a room wearing the shortest skirt and the highest heels and then another woman can enter wearing a tracksuit, but the woman in the tracksuit could look a slut purely by the way she carries herself. When I go to a club, I want to look nice, like a lady and feel a bit sexy. But the rest of the time I'm in sweats and look like shit.

99

Britney, on attracting attention for the type of clothes she wears, *FHM* magazine, 29 September 2000.

66

At first, I found the fame and attention and the workload overwhelming. It was very weird, especially because I was of the age where my hormones were flying around and I didn't just have people at school talking about me, I had the whole world on my back. That was kind of hard to come to terms with.

99

Britney, on becoming famous aged 17, *FHM* magazine, 29 September 2000.

> **"**
> I do pray every night –
> well, I try to pray every
> night. I pray to be a better
> person. Have I ever been
> sneaky and prayed for a
> number one? Sometimes!
> **"**

Britney, on praying, *Smash Hits* magazine, 17 May 2000.

66

I want someone who loves me for me, not for being 'Britney the pop star'. He's got to be able to make me laugh, and he's got to be up for having a lot of fun, but at the same time he has to understand what I do and everything that goes with it. I don't go for any particular look though; I like all different types of boys!

99

Britney, on her perfect boyfriend, *Smash Hits* magazine, 17 May 2000.

Justin Timberlake's cute nickname for Britney was "Pinky". (She called him "Stinky".)

"

I don't think God will punish me because I don't go to church every Sunday. He's looking at my circumstances and he realizes I can't.

"

Britney, on going to church, *Top of the Pops* magazine, 5 May 2000.

66

I think people forget I'm still only 17 and they can still say things to hurt my feelings.

99

Britney, on the media being unkind,
Big magazine, 4 August 1999.

66

I wouldn't have dressed like that in a teenage magazine, but *Rolling Stone* is an edgy publication. I thought it was fine – it wasn't like I was wearing a bathing suit. I think it's good to see myself in a different way.

99

Britney, on that infamous skimpy *Rolling Stone* photoshoot, *FHM* magazine, 1 July 1999.

"

It doesn't mean physically hit me. It means just give me a sign, basically. I think it's kind of funny that people would actually think that's what it meant.

"

Britney, on the meaning behind "hit me" in "Baby One More Time", interview by Stephen Daly, *Rolling Stone*, 15 April 1999.

66

All I did was tie up my shirt! I'm wearing a sports bra under it. Sure, I'm wearing thigh-highs, but kids wear those – it's the style. Have you seen MTV – all those in thongs?

99

Britney, on the Catholic schoolgirl outfit controversy, interview by Stephen Daly, *Rolling Stone*, 15 April 1999.

66

I feel like the simple Southern morals were instilled in me, as far as I know who I am, and I know where I come from. I still believe in saying "yes, ma'am" and "no, ma'am" in the traditional ways of how they do it in the South. I try to keep a foundation of that in my household.

99

Britney, on her Southern morals, *In Style* magazine, 10 December 2013.

> **"**
> I like to believe there is a little magic in the world, but I also believe we choose our own path.
> **"**

Britney, on destiny, *V* magazine, 3 March 2011.

66

This is going to sound weird – I walk around my house naked. I've always been very comfortable being nude. Since I was a little girl. And it's not like I was trying to be sexual or anything, it's just a safe feeling for me to be nude. I don't feel like I have anything to hide.

99

Britney, on her love of being naked, *Q* magazine, 30 September 2006.

66

Anyone can sit down and
write some boring artistic
song. Pop music is the
hardest shit to write.

99

Britney, on writing pop songs, *Entertainment Weekly*,
9 May 2003.

"

When I met with Madonna, I was a freak – a freak! Like, I went in there and, like, something came over my body and I got really, really nervous and I walked in, and I said, 'I feel like I should hug you!' What was I thinking? I'm just like this country hillbilly that needs to go back to Louisiana.

"

Britney, on meeting Madonna for the first time, *Popstar!* magazine, 19 November 2001.

"
Sometimes I wonder
if there's something
wrong with me, because
I don't think it's bad
to show my belly.

"

Britney, on baring her midriff in videos and photo
shoots, *YM* magazine, 21 September 2001.

Britney's audition tape, sent to future-manager Larry Rudolph in 1997, included a cover performance of Whitney Houston's "I Have Nothing".

It alone secured her a record deal.

66

The press will ask me things like what's the worst thing I've done sexually. I'm not going to go there. Why do they care anyway?

99

Britney, on the press going too far, *YM* magazine, 21 September 2001.

> **"** I do miss being able to have a personal life. There always seems to be a photographer watching you or a journalist waiting with their pen at the ready to catch you out. **"**

Britney, on being too famous, *Disney Adventures* magazine, 30 April 2001.

Britney began songwriting for her third album, *Britney*. In order to keep track of the melodies and lyrics she wrote when away on tour, she would call her house's telephone number in Louisiana and leave a message on her answering machine.

The first song she wrote herself was 'Not a Girl, Not Yet a Woman'.

"

I think all teenagers want
to feel sexy. There's
nothing wrong with that.

"

Britney, on her sexuality, *TV Guide*, 3 June 2000.

66

In the town where I live, everyone thinks of me as just plain ol' Britney.

99

Britney, on people back home in Louisiana,
Smash Hits magazine, 2 May 2000.

"

I love to just get in my car and ride. And listen to music. I'm in my own world, and it's the best experience.

"

Britney, on her favourite type of down time, *Teen* magazine, 10 August 1999.

❝

I basically just want my life back. I want to be able to drive my car. I want to be able to live in my house by myself.

❞

Britney, on the confines of her conservatorship, interview by Jenny Eliscu, *Rolling Stone*, 28 November 2011.

66

I think I'm still clean living. I mean I don't go home and have orgies or anything like that. I'm still the same person I've always been.

99

Britney, on life after fame, interview with Tucker Carlson, CNN, 4 September 2003.

❝

Larry Rudolph [her future manager] told my dad, 'Pop music is coming back. Send me a tape of Britney singing.'

❞

Britney, on her first audition tape, which landed her a record deal, *Entertainment Weekly*, 5 March 1999.

> **"**
> It made more sense to go pop, because I can dance to it – it's more me.
> **"**

Britney, discussing the direction she wanted to take her debut record, interview with Stephen Daly, *Rolling Stone*, May 1999.

"
The cool thing about being famous is travelling. I have always wanted to travel across seas. Like, to Canada, and stuff.

"

Britney, on travelling, *The Guardian*, 14 September 2008.

CHAPTER
TWO

ORIGINAL DOLL

In 2004, Britney recorded another album back-to-back with *In the Zone*, a secret known to not that many. It was a dark, "forbidden" and contemplative album that expressed her profound personal sadness that the world would soon see splashed across the tabloids. Her record label wouldn't allow her to release it – a foreshadowing of her scramble to control her own career and future. "Original Doll" is a title that elegantly sums up how Britney felt about herself. Let's explore the darker, dangerous side of Britney…

> **"**
> To be honest, I just wanted
> to get into the Top 40 in
> the US – so when my single
> and album went to number
> one, I couldn't believe it! I
> was like, 'Oh my goodness!'
> **"**

Britney, on her incredible debut success, *TV Hits*
magazine, 9 July 1999.

Britney joined the Disney Channel's *All New Mickey Mouse Club* TV show, which included fellow future A-list celebrities such as Christina Aguilera, Ryan Gosling and Justin Timberlake. She was 11 years old.

66

I listen to a lot of different music from all over the world and I guess I just gravitate towards what sounds fresh and what makes me want to move. I really didn't want to record anything on this album that could be mistaken for anyone else out there.

99

Britney, on her album recording process, *Rolling Stone*, 17 March 2011.

66

Ma'am, I'm not here to be anyone's slave.

99

Britney's statement to Judge Brenda Penny, U.S. Court, regarding her conservatorship, 23 June 2021.

66

I care more about feeling sexy than looking sexy. That all comes from within.

99

Britney, on feeling sexy, interview by Louise Gannon, *Marie Claire UK*, 1 September 2016.

"

Vegas is definitely a new challenge. But I wanted to be able to put on a different type of show. You get to do so much more when you don't have to put your stage in trucks after the show every night – we got to build a venue specifically for my show. It's going to be more like a party than a concert.

"

Britney, on her famous Planet Hollywood Las Vegas Residency, interview with Peter Robinson, *Stella* magazine, 28 January 2014.

66

I feel like an old person now. I go to bed at 9:30 every night, and I don't go out or anything. I just feel like an old fart.

99

Britney, on her conservatorship, interview by Jenny Eliscu, *Rolling Stone*, 28 November 2011.

In 2000, Britney had the music video idea for her latest single, "Oops! I Did It Again". "I want to be dancing on Mars. I want to be in a red latex jumpsuit. I want to have a really cute spaceman.... but there can't be any rockets," she told MTV in 2002.

> **"**
> I think generally people probably see me as a sweety goody two shoes and that's cool: at heart that's how I am. But I do have a wild side.
> **"**

Britney, on her wild side, interview by Jo Elvin, *Glamour* magazine, 20 March 2003.

66

It's pop music, but it's definitely different. I've changed, and this album reflects how my tastes in music have changed. I think if you keep challenging yourself to do something different, people will see that and like that. But it's up to me to change. And I can't sing the same kind of thing all the time. That would bore me.

99

Britney, on her second album *Oops! I Did It Again*, interview by Jenny Eliscu, *The Observer*, 16 September 2001.

66

It doesn't look like I have fake boobs, does it? I mean, of course they're real.

99

Britney, on the breast implant rumour made up by the media, *Cosmo GIRL*, 31 May 2000.

66

Check in with yourself every day cause things can get really crazy. You need to do normal things to stay sane – I see a lot of my friends when I go home and it's still completely normal. We all grew up together so we're like sisters – I would kick their butts if they kissed my butt.

99

Britney, on how to stay normal when things get crazy, *Big* magazine, 4 August 1999.

In 2012, Britney was a judge on the second season of *The X Factor* in the U.S. She was reportedly paid $15 million for one season's appearance, becoming the highest-paid celebrity judge in TV history!

66

I think police officers' uniforms are sexy. Maybe in my next video, I'll be a police officer. And I could be shooting all the paparazzi! That's a great idea! I love it!

99

Britney, on paparazzi, Q magazine, 30 September 2006.

"

When you perform, you have to be dangerous.

"

Britney, on her live performances, *Harper's Bazaar*, 17 July 2006.

On 16 February 2007, after demanding that her then-ex-husband let her see her children, and being allegedly refused, Britney drove to a random Los Angeles hair salon and asked to have her head shaved.

When the hairdresser said no, Britney grabbed the clippers and did it herself. "I just don't want anybody touching my head. I don't want anyone touching my hair. I'm sick of people touching my hair," she gave as the reason.

"

No matter what I wear, critics are going to say something, so I just wear what I want! At the end of the day, I'll wear what I think is cute. One of the cool things about being a celebrity is that it's like playing dress-up every day!

"

Britney, on being a celebrity, *M* magazine, 15 July 2002.

66

I don't think I'm a sexually provocative performer. I really just get into what I do, and maybe, yeah, I may wear something that shows my belly, but other than that I haven't done anything that crazy. Like, I haven't masturbated on a bed!

99

Britney, on being like Madonna, interview with Jonathan Van Meter, *Vogue*, 31 October 2001.

66

Underneath, I'm a real goody-goody. I was brought up with high moral values, but there's a part of me that likes to look and act bad. It's like playing dress-up. Why do I have to be an angel or devil all the time? That would be boring.

99

Britney, discussing her high moral values,
YM magazine, 21 September 2001.

"

If I brush my hair the wrong way, people are going to talk. And I expect that. But I hate it when the people around me start giving in to what the public says.

"

Britney, on being the subject of media obsession, *Allure* magazine, 29 April 2000.

> **"**
> I have a picture of Brad Pitt on my refrigerator, and I kiss him every morning!
> **"**

Britney, on her main teen squeeze, *Teen* magazine, 10 August 1999.

"
My prerogative right now is to just chill and let all the other overexposed blondes on the cover of *US Weekly* be your entertainment.
"

Britney, on taking a break after her knee injury, interview by Gary Susman, *Entertainment Weekly*, 18 October 2004.

> **"**
> I didn't know it was going
> to be that long and
> everything... but it was cool.
> **"**

Britney, on her onstage kiss with Madonna, interview
with Tucker Carlson, CNN, 4 September 2003.

"

I'm a mature person, a lot of people say I have an old soul. But at the same time, you've gotta stay young and not always be so serious all the time. I can still be goofy and silly – it's always good to just crack up, do something really stupid and just not care.

"

Britney, on growing up so quickly in the music industry, *Smash Hits* Interview, 12 January 2000.

Britney started singing into her hairbrush when she was just two years old. Her debut performance was singing the Christmas carol 'What Child Is This' at her kindergarten graduation. A star was born!

"

I know this may sound silly, but when I was younger, I was never really insecure. At all. Never. Now I get insecure when I go places because people expect celebrities to look a certain way. And there are mornings I wake up and my butt feels fat.

"

Britney, on her insecurities, interview by Jenny Eliscu, *The Observer*, 16 September 2001.

66

Justin is such a sweetheart. He is everything, and what more could you want in a person? He's funny. He's cute. He's great. He just understands. I get him and he gets me, and that's cool.

99

Britney, on her first big famous relationship, with Justin Timberlake, Teen People Awards, 10 February 2001.

"

I was in shock, to be honest. I didn't know what to say, what to do. That was the last thing I ever thought somebody might do. I was really shocked shitless. But you live and you learn.

"

Britney, on being the controversial subject of Justin Timberlake's 'Cry Me A River' music video, interview by Mark Binelli, *Rolling Stone*, 2 October 2003.

> 66
>
> I think a lot of the things I've done that seemed absurd were out of rebellion and out of wanting to break free. I know that sounds weird, but I can't live in a prison.
>
> 99

Britney, on being herself, interview with Deborah Baer, *Seventeen* magazine, 31 March 2004.

66

I kissed a bunch of frogs and finally found my prince.

99

Britney, on then-husband Kevin Federline,
People magazine, 13 August 2004.

66

Hopefully my sons will respect me by the way I carry myself, and in doing that, they will know how to respect other women.

99

Britney, on her children, *Glamour* magazine, 29 November 2008.

66

It's the music I make which will keep people's interest.

99

Britney, on keeping her fans interested,
Smash Hits Interview, 23 February 2000.

CHAPTER
THREE

FEMME
FATALE

From squeaky-clean Southerner to 24/7/365 work bitch, right on through to frankly-downright-flesh-obsessed femme fatale, Britney grew up in front of her fans' eyes, transforming into the complex, creative and contradictory artist we know and love today – and a million miles away from that "pop puppet" everyone (wrongly) assumed she was. What a journey it was... Let's dive in to take a closer look...

"
The bitch is back and better than ever!

"

Britney, on how she would describe her album,
Femme Fatale, *V* magazine, 3 March 2011.

"

A woman who is sexy and strong, dangerous and mysterious, cool and confident.

"

Britney, on defining a femme fatale, *V magazine*, 3 March 2011.

"

It's so sad that as soon as you start doing all the things you ever dreamed of you end up obsessing about how little sleep you're getting. I feel like an old fart.

"

Britney, on the draining demands of touring, *FHM* magazine, 29 September 2000.

"

Everything I have ever done – even my movie – I helped to write it; the whole idea came from me. All my shows and all my tours and everything. They're all of me and I'm so the complete opposite (to a puppet). But people still say, 'Oh, she's just pretty. She was just given that song. She's a puppet.' It's really bizarre.

"

Britney, on being considered a puppet in the music industry, interview by Jo Elvin, *Glamour* magazine, 20 March 2003.

In 1997, Britney was an original member of the girl-group Innosense – the American answer to the Spice Girls. However, her ambitions to be a solo artist shone too bright, and she signed a record deal with Jive Records the same year.

Ironically, the highlight of Innosense's career, before disbanding, was opening for Britney at a few concerts in 2000.

❝

It's mind-blowing to have a child. I think it's kind of healing too. All the secrets from your family come out of the closet for some reason. But it's good. They have to come out sometime. You know what I mean?

❞

Britney, on becoming a mother, interview by Holly Millea, *Elle* magazine, 6 September 2005.

"

The control my father
had over someone as
powerful as me – he loved
the control to hurt his
own daughter 100,000
per cent. He loved it.

"

Britney's statement to Judge Brenda Penny, U.S. Court,
regarding her conservatorship, 23 June 2021.

❝

I worked seven days a week, no days off, which in California, the only similar thing to this is called sex trafficking. Making anyone work against their will, taking all their possessions away and placing them in a home where they work with the people who live with them. They watched me change every day – morning, noon and night. I had no privacy; I gave eight gallons of blood a week.

❞

Britney's statement to the Judge Brenda Penny, U.S. Court, regarding her conservatorship, 23 June 2021.

"

I tried taking a break once. I announced that I was taking a year off. It lasted three weeks. I have so much energy, I need to keep busy. I need to be working all the time. It feels normal to me. It feels healthy.

"

Britney, on being a work bitch (to use her phrase), *Entertainment Weekly*, 21 November 2003.

"

Having sex is a really big deal and should not be dealt with lightly – it's not only a physical thing but an emotional one, too. I believe that it's something you should experience for the first time in the union of marriage.

"

Britney, on sex before marriage, *Smash Hits* magazine, 3 October 2001.

"

I definitely would not miss having my picture taken everywhere I go. I wouldn't miss showering in arenas either. So gross!

"

Britney, when asked what she wouldn't miss if her fame ended tomorrow, *V* magazine, 3 March 2011.

"

A critic's job is to criticize somebody and what kind of job is that? My main focus is that my fans are happy.... not some 40-year-old fart!

"

Britney, on critics, *M* magazine, 15 July 2002.

66

I think people look at me and think that I have it so easy, and that all of this is glamorous. I mean, it's fun, but it's hard work.

99

Britney, on working hard, *16* magazine,
10 September 2000.

66

I miss being able to do normal things and not have people stare at me all the time. Just going to a restaurant and having people expecting you to smile – there are days when, just like anybody else, you don't want to talk. You just want to be by yourself, and people get the wrong idea. They think you're a snob.

99

Britney, on the downsides of fame, *Allure* magazine, 29 April 2000.

"

Why are they not going after Christina Aguilera? Have they seen what she has on? I know I'm acting like a four-year-old right now, but Beyoncé dresses provocatively. Why don't they say something about her? What is too sexy to them? My family, we walked around the house naked, we really did. By the time I was 13, my dad was like, 'Uh, Britney, it's time to start covering yourself up.' I'm very free like that.

"

Britney, on being slut-shamed by the media, interview with Lorraine Ali, *Newsweek*, 3 November 2003.

"

I don't live a completely normal life because I'm not, you know, a typical teenager who goes to school every day. But I try to make it as normal as possible.

"

Britney, on trying to be a normal teenager, *Teen* magazine, 10 August 1999.

66

I don't like to think about that. I don't want to be part of someone's *Lolita* thing. It kind of freaks me out.

99

Britney, on her older male fans, interview with Chris Mundy, *Rolling Stone*, 25 May 2000.

66

I view people like presents. There are some with uglier wrapping paper and there are others with beautiful wrapping, but it's the gift inside that matters.

99

Britney, on being a gift, *Tiger Beat* magazine, 30 August 2000.

> **"**
> Every little thing I do is always scrutinized. 'Overprotected' was a song I wrote about being tired of trying to please everyone and not being able to just be me.
> **"**

Britney, on 'Overprotected', *YM* magazine, 21 September 2001.

"

We worked together on the video for my song 'Slumber Party'. I kept his number and a few months later gave him a call. The simple things that are most meaningful – I'm a romantic. I believe in love, so I'm open to my marriage.

"

Britney, on meeting her husband Sam Asghari, *ES Interview* magazine, 2 August 2018.

> **"**
> Number 14 in *FHM*'s Sexiest Women in the World? I'm really flattered. This is the first list like that I've ever been in, although I was voted 'most beautiful' in my high school yearbook.
> **"**

Britney, on being voted beautiful in a men's magazine, *FHM* magazine, 1 July 1999.

66

Yes, I was asked to meet Prince William, but it didn't work out. I would love to have met up, but the press got hold of it and it was cancelled. Which is probably a blessing because had we met up, I would have never been left alone by the press.

99

Britney, on dating Prince William rumours, *FHM* magazine, 29 September 2000.

"

It's funny, I hate to say it, but I love reading *US Weekly*, I love reading *Star* magazine. It's entertaining to me, because the stuff is so not true. It's, like, the other day, they had this huge article about me finding a hair in my sandwich. We were sitting there laughing for eight hours about that shit.

"

Britney, on U.S. celebrity gossip magazines, interview by Mark Binelli, *Rolling Stone*, 2 October 2003.

66

I'm a big vibe person when it comes to music, so a song really has to make me feel a certain way in order for me to fall in love with it. I love hard pounding dance songs with really beautiful melodies over them. Those are my favourites.

99

Britney, on songs she likes to write and record, *Rolling Stone*, 17 March 2011.

66

All I want is to own my money, for this to end, and my boyfriend to drive me in his fucking car.

99

Britney's statement to Judge Brenda Penny, U.S. Court, regarding her conservatorship, 23 June 2021.

66

I would honestly like to sue my family, to be totally honest with you. I also would like to be able to share my story with the world, and what they did to me, instead of it being a hush-hush secret to benefit all of them.

99

Britney's statement to Judge Brenda Penny, U.S. Court, regarding her conservatorship, 23 June 2021.

"

If I make good music, then I can't go wrong. I want to be around for a long time. As long as I'm happy and I'm having fun. And who's to say next year that I won't hate this? I don't think I ever will – music is where my heart is. But as far as the business side of things? I don't like it. Like the press and stuff. It's so horrible.

"

Britney, on the media and music industry,
Teen magazine, 29 July 2001.

"

I won't take BS from anyone. And I think it's making me stand out on my own and be very independent and fight for what I believe in. Whereas before I was a young, blonde girl who would do what she was told. I know who I am as a person and I'm getting damn strong.

"

Britney, on standing up for herself, interview with Matt Lauer, *Dateline*, 16 June 2006.

66

At first, gossip hurt me because as a teenager you have to deal with issues like that in school, people talking about you. But now I have the whole world talking about me!

99

Britney, on tabloid rumours, *M* magazine, 15 July 2002.

> **"**
> Justin tells me I look
> prettiest without
> makeup. I'm like, 'Yeah,
> right. Whatever!'
> **"**

Britney, on Justin Timberlake, *YM* magazine,
21 September 2001.

" Most days I pop into Starbucks to grab a coffee or a Frappuccino. There's always a queue and I just wait my turn. I don't like it when I get special treatment, as I feel embarrassed. Calm down, I'm not the President! **"**

Britney, on fame, *Disney Adventures* magazine, 30 April 2001.

66

Trust me, I'm only human, I can be a bitch. But I value the person who'll come up and say, 'Look, Britney, you're being a bitch.'

99

Britney, on her bad moods, *Smash Hits* magazine, 2 May 2000.

66

I just say, 'Fe [Britney's former assistant], it's stormy outside,' and she knows to clear everyone away and let me be by myself.

99

Britney, on having her own down time, interview with Chris Mundy, *Rolling Stone*, 25 May 2000.

"

I've never really wanted to go to Japan, simply because I don't like eating fish and I know that's very popular out there in Africa.

"

Britney, confused as to where Japan is, *The Guardian*, 14 September 2008.

66

I was so nervous because it was already out that a *girl* was opening up for 'N Sync. I'd walk out there and my first two performances, they were like, 'Booooo'. Once I'd start performing, they'd go…*crazy*.

99

Britney, on supporting 'N Sync at the start of her career, *Entertainment Weekly*, 5 March 1999.

66

The best gift your parents can give you is to let you go out into the world and mess up, because it's allowing you to be free and learn who you are. And I think that's a cool thing, to make mistakes sometimes. You do learn a lot about yourself.

99

Britney, on her parents, interview with Deborah Baer, *Seventeen* magazine, 31 March 2004.

CHAPTER
FOUR

IT'S BRITNEY, BITCH

In 2007, on her track 'Gimme More', Britney gave the world perhaps her most iconic and inspirational statement of intent – a phrase that defined her comeback following her very public meltdown and rebranded her as a savvy showgirl. "I have come back so many times, people are just like, 'Is this another one?' It's kind of like a joke to me now," Britney told *Glamour* magazine in 2008. But it's Britney, bitch, she can do what she likes!

66

It's a really small town. Only about two thousand people live there so everyone knows everyone else, which is really cool. There are a lot of cows there but not much else. And it's a 15-minute drive to the nearest McDonald's!

99

Britney, discussing her hometown, Kentwood, Louisiana, *Top of the Pops* magazine, 3 May 1999.

"

Some people have said my first two albums sound similar, but that's just my sound. I think it's cool that I have my own sound. No one can touch that – I'm marking my own territory, and this is the music I sing.

"

Britney, on her unique sound, *16* magazine, 10 September 2000.

66

I'm all up for a joke. There are so many cracks about me, you have to laugh it off and make a joke about it. Otherwise, you'll drive yourself crazy.

99

Britney, on not taking fame too seriously,
Teen People Awards, 10 February 2001.

"

I think 90 per cent of the world would agree that the tabloids have kind of gone a little far with me lately.

"

Britney, on tabloid rumours, interview with Matt Lauer, *Dateline*, 16 June 2006.

66

I'm not going to walk around in hot pants and a bra on the street, but when you're an artist you sometimes play a part.

99

Britney, on playing a part, *16 Superstars* magazine, 30 April 2000.

"

Even when you go to jail, you know there's the time when you're gonna get out. But in this situation, it's never ending. It's just like *Groundhog Day* every day. If I wasn't under the restraints I'm under, I'd feel so liberated.

"

Britney, on the confines of her conservatorship, interview by Jenny Eliscu, *Rolling Stone*, 28 November 2011.

> **Ma'am, my dad and anyone involved in this conservatorship and my management who played a huge role in punishing me when I said no – ma'am, they should be in jail.**

Britney's statement to Judge Brenda Penny, U.S. Court, regarding her conservatorship, 23 June 2021.

"

I'm sorry that my life seemed like it was all over the place the past two years, it's probably because it was! Going and going and going is all I've ever known since I was 15 years old. It's amazing what advisors will push you to do, even if it means taking a naïve, young, blonde girl and putting her on the cover of every magazine.

"

Britney, on working hard, interview by Gary Sussman, *Entertainment Weekly*, 18 October 2004.

"

I genuinely love to sing and dance. When I get in a creative mood, I can't shut up; it's the craziest thing. At one point I was thinking of being a home mum, but when my son sees me dance, he lights up. Then I know what I'm supposed to be doing – if Mom's happy, baby's happy!

"

Britney, on her work–life balance, interview by Jane Bussmann, *Glamour* magazine, 10 May 2006.

> **"**
> What I do know now is that I don't believe in the happy ever after. I just believe in happy right now. And I'm very grateful for that.
> **"**

Britney, on relationships, interview by Louise Gannon, *Marie Claire UK*, 1 September 2016.

"

My family ruined my dreams 100 billion percent and try to make me look like the crazy one. My family loves to pull me down and hurt me, always, so I am disgusted with them!

"

Britney, on her family, Twitter, 14 January 2021.

66

'Touch of My Hand' is probably the one song that's a little graphic. It's about indulging in yourself, taking off your clothes and feeling kind of good. Definitely get the candles out for that one! But there's nothing about it I would personally find distasteful.

99

Britney, on the sexually suggestive elements of some of her songs, *Entertainment Weekly*, 21 November 2003.

"

I secretly long for piercings and tattoos! I really don't know where I'd have another piercing, but I'd never have one... you know... down there!

"

Britney, on tattoos and piercing, *Top of the Pops* magazine, 5 May 2000.

66

I like music that makes you move and connects with your soul. I like to feel inspired right away when I listen to new music. I always have songs being sent to me from new artists and producers from all over the world, which is really cool. From there I just follow my heart.

99

Britney, on how she chooses which songs to make her own, *V* magazine, 3 March 2011.

"

If not, then God definitely has a strange sense of humour.

"

Britney, when asked if she was destined to be a star, *V* magazine, 3 March 2011.

"

No, Larry [her manager], you don't understand. I'm scared because I'm not nervous at all. And that just doesn't seem right.

"

Britney, on hosting that now-iconic *Saturday Night Live*, interview with Jonathan Van Meter, *Vogue*, 31 October 2001.

66

I'm not a fake person, and the fans probably appreciate that. At this age, you want someone to relate to, especially being a teenager, having all these insecurities.

99

Britney, on being real for her fans,
Teen People Awards, 10 February 2001.

66

I like *Crossroads*! Fuck you!

99

Britney, on her critically panned movie *Crossroads*,
interview with Peter Robinson, *Stella* magazine,
28 January 2014.

CHAPTER
FIVE

BRIT POP

Britney's bubble burst in 2007 when she had a very public mental health breakdown that saw the singer's life descend into madness. No one knew if Britney would ever bounce back, and when her father enforced a strict conservatorship on her, the world cried tears for Ms. Spears – a cry that would ultimately lead to the #freebritney movement that set her free, finally, *thirteen years* later.

"

Oh my God, I'm over the belly thing. I'm never showing my belly again.

"

Britney, on showing her midriff in the "Baby One More Time" video, *The Guardian*, 14 September 2008.

"

The first day of making the video for 'Oops! I Did It Again' was fine. I had a red vinyl catsuit on and it made me look completely flat, so I had to wear those fake boobs. But then they started falling down and I was so humiliated! We ended up having to sew them in. The catsuit was extremely hot: It got to the point where the sweat was coming out of the sleeves when I'd swing my arms around. It was so gross! We did that dance number 15 million times.

"

Britney, on that iconic red latex jumpsuit for the "Oops! I Did It Again" video, *Allure* magazine, 29 April 2000.

66

Everything I do is my idea. Just because I'm young, people think I'm controlled by someone else. I come up with all of my video concepts, and I want the respect for it. If you want to know what I'm going through, just listen to my music. I'm writing almost every song now. I had to do that for me.

99

Britney, on being in control of her career, *YM* magazine, 21 September 2001.

66

The press like to have the person they pick on. I feel like I'm a target and I feel like other girls are. At a certain point in everybody's career, they'll get it.

99

Britney, on being hounded by the media,
interview with Matt Lauer, *Dateline*, 16 June 2006.

66

I'd definitely date a garbage man! You know, if I fell in love with him, or like a guy who worked in McDonald's. I'd have to be with him whoever he was. I'd have to follow my heart.

99

Britney, on following her heart to find love, *Top of the Pops* magazine, 5 May 2000.

> **"**
> The biggest mistake
> I've ever made? To not
> trust my instincts.
> **"**

Britney, on her instincts, interview with
Peter Robinson, PopJustice, 28 January 2014.

66

I wanted to feel that it came from me. I've written more on this album than any other album. I wanted to put out a piece of me.

99

Britney, on her ninth studio album, *Glory*, interview by Louise Gannon, *Marie Claire UK*, 1 September 2016.

> 66
>
> I've lied and told the whole world 'I'm okay. And I'm happy.' It's a lie. I've been in shock. I am traumatized. But now I'm telling you the truth. Okay? I'm not happy. I can't sleep. I'm so angry. It's insane. And I'm depressed. I cry every day.
>
> 99

Britney's statement to Judge Brenda Penny, U.S. Court, regarding her conservatorship, 23 June 2021.

"

I've always followed my heart and pursued my dreams, and I imagine that people find that inspiring. I hope that is the effect I have on my fans and people in general. I definitely want to project a positive energy out into the world.

"

Britney, on how she'd like to be remembered, interview with Peter Robinson, *Stella* magazine, 28 January 2014.

66

Some of the songs maybe weren't that great. But they were light-hearted, and they were me at that time, you know what I mean? It's like when you look at a photo album from when you were younger, and you say, 'What was I thinking wearing that?'

99

Britney, on her first album, *YM* magazine, 10 September 2000.

> **"**
>
> My mom was freaking out. She was like, 'Oh, my God, my daughter can sing!' And from then on, I started doing competitions and winning a lot.
>
> **"**

Britney, on her mom first hearing her singing voice, interview with Jonathan Van Meter, *Vogue*, 31 October 2001.

66

I try to be me. Where I'm from, in the South, it's unheard of for girls to go out and do their own thing, but my mom was like, "You can do freakin' anything." Instead of looking up to other people, I wish girls would have their own dreams and freakin' go for them.

99

Britney, on life goals, *YM* magazine, 21 September 2001.

"

I try to act tough but I'm
not. I want all of this...
but it's not always easy.

"

Britney, on fame and fortune, interview by
Louise Gannon, *Marie Claire UK*, 1 September 2016.

"
Well, I'm not a man.

"

Britney, telling a journalist what she was if not a girl, not yet a woman, *The Guardian*, 14 September 2008.

CHAPTER
SIX

A WOMAN NO LONGER A GIRL

From perfect pop princess to toxic womanizer, edgy disconaut to risky R&B rebel, Britney is a chameleon of popular culture, beloved by her army of fans. She's all grown up now, in her forties, a woman no longer a girl. What's next for our Brit is *up to her*…so let's jump into her wonderful world and hit her up… one…more….time…and be thankful she survived all the chaos and craziness.

66

I think just being pure and doing nothing to destroy your body is cool. I think that's what's in right now.

99

Britney, on remaining pure until marriage, *Teen* magazine, 10 August 1999.

66

People assume I'm some puppet and people are telling me what to do all the time. When I first got signed to a record label, I was 15. So, I did have some help at first. You don't know what you're doing. But now, with experience and as time goes on, I know exactly what I need.

99

Britney, on growing up in the industry, USA Weekend, 18 February 2000.

"

I would really, really,
really like to be a legend
like Madonna.

"

Britney, on Madonna, *Allure* magazine, 29 April 2000.

66

The kids are great. But the forty-something men can be… space invaders.

99

Britney, on young and old fans, *Allure* magazine, 29 April 2000.

"

I always have melodies in my head. Usually in the bathtub, I'll be playing around with melodies and ideas.

"

Britney, on songwriting, interview with Chris Mundy, *Rolling Stone*, 25 May 2000.

"

When people start telling me how big I am, I don't want to talk about it. It's something that scares me for some reason. I don't know why.

"

Britney, on her level of fame, Teen People Awards, 10 February 2001.

Britney's first perfume, *Curious*, was released in 2004. It has notes of Louisiana magnolia – from where Britney grew up – as well as golden Anjou pear, lotus flower, tuberose, star jasmine, pink cyclamen, vanilla-infused musk, sandalwood and blonde woods.

To date, Britney has released more than 30 perfumes.

66
Bubbly, innocent, respectable, fun and responsible.

99

Britney, describing herself in five words,
Disney Adventures magazine, 30 April 2001.

"

Sometimes you wanna be sexy and bad, like Samantha. Then you wanna be vulnerable like Charlotte. Or the one who analyzes everything – Carrie. Or just be so together, like Miranda. *Sex and the City* is my favourite show in the whole world.

"

Britney, on her favourite TV show, *YM* magazine, 21 September 2001.

66

If right now we got in the car and went to Starbucks you would see 20 photographers there. They're coming up on the sides of the car which is a scary situation for me. And they're banging on the windows and that's not something I want my baby to see, so I go home.

99

Britney, on being hounded by the media, interview with Matt Lauer, *Dateline*, 16 June 2006.

66

I don't think I thought about fame when I was a child. I knew I wanted to perform, and I knew I wanted to be on stage, but I don't think I ever thought about fame or what comes with being famous.

99

Britney, on fame, *V* magazine, 3 March 2011.

There is a part of me in my music and I hope, for my fans, that they can have that part of me when they hear me on the radio, or buy my CD, or whatever they do.

Britney, on music being a piece of her, interview by Gregg LaGambina, *Flaunt* magazine, 8 September 2016.

66

What I feed off are new challenges and different performances. Just being on stage and having all those people out there is just the most adrenalin-filled, just the best feeling in the world. That's something I'll never lose.

99

Britney, on her love of performing live,
Smash Hits interview, 12 January 2000.

66

I'm focused when I'm in the studio writing or on stage doing a sound check. But afterwards I have time to go a little crazy – you have to get all that negative energy out and go a little mad.

99

Britney, on shaking off the stress of being a superstar, *Top of the Pops* magazine, 5 May 2000.

> **"** In the bathroom I could sing more songs because it echoed. It was when I got out of the tub and started singing in front of my parents that I would just totally get on their nerves! **"**

Britney, on finding her voice as a youngster,
YM magazine, 10 September 2000.

"

In so many interviews they make me sound either really stupid and ditzy, or very snobbish. I'm really down-to-earth and kind of shy. I'm just confident on stage.

"

Britney, on interviews and performing live,
Teen magazine, 29 July 2001.

In 20 years at the top, Britney has won almost every music award going: a Grammy, six MTV Video Music Awards, an MTV Lifetime Achievement Award, nine Billboard Music Awards, three World Music Awards, eight Teen Choice Awards, and even a star on the Hollywood Walk of Fame – at age 21, the youngest singer ever to do so.

❝

I think sometimes, because I'm from the South, there's a misconception. Girls from the South are really nice, so people think we're pushovers. You know? We know how to work it – it's about being a lady and still getting what you want.

❞

Britney, on being from the South, interview by Jo Elvin, *Glamour* magazine, 20 March 2003.

With her then-husband, Kevin Federline, Britney starred in a short-lived reality TV show, aptly called *Chaotic*.

"I would never do something like that again," she said of the ordeal. "Actually, it was probably the worst thing I've done in my career."

66

I did party a little bit. But what the hell else am I gonna do? I'm a teenager. Of course, I experimented in that I partied... and stuff. But that's not me.

99

Britney, on rumours of wild partying, interview by Mark Binelli, *Rolling Stone*, 2 October 2003.

66

People made such a big deal out of it. I honestly don't get it. It's weird. To me, the human body is beautiful.

99

Britney, on that iconic onstage kiss with Madonna, *Entertainment Weekly* magazine, 21 November 2003.

"

The naughtiest thing I ever did? I did it on my boyfriend.

"

Britney, on being naughty, interview by Jane Bussmann, *Glamour* magazine, 10 May 2006.

66

Sometimes it's our secrets that define us.

99

Britney, being elusive, interview with Peter Robinson, PopJustice, 28 January 2014.

66
I constantly want to outdo
the last thing I've done.
99

Britney, on her thirst for success, interview with
Peter Robinson, PopJustice, 28 January 2014.

> **"**
> I never go to 'the club'.
> But I think it's fun to sing
> about it. And I have my own
> mini club at my house.
> **"**

Britney, on clubbing, interview with Peter Robinson,
PopJustice, 28 January 2014.

In 2013, Britney began a Las Vegas residency at Planet Hollywood. Often regarded as the final resting place of "where old musicians go to die", it was Britney's spectacular show that transformed the fortunes of Vegas; the Strip now attracts contemporary superstar performers.

To acknowledge this fact, in 2014 Las Vegas declared every 5 November "Britney Day".

"

You put yourself through it again and again. But each time love takes you over. It feels different every time for me. Every guy who I've been with, it's been a different kind of love.

"

Britney, on falling in love, interview with Peter Robinson, *Stella* magazine, 28 January 2014.

66

I have lots of incredible in my life, but no normal.

99

Britney, on living a life less ordinary, interview by Louise Gannon, *Marie Claire UK*, 1 September 2016.

> **"**
> My kids completely understand that the person I am on stage is an act and it's not Mom. I don't think they think I'm in any way special. They just think that's my job.
> **"**

Britney, on her kids, interview by Louise Gannon, *Marie Claire UK*, 1 September 2016.

Crossroads, Britney's first foray into leading-lady territory in a full-length feature film, was written by newcomer, Shonda Rhimes.

Rhimes went on to create *Grey's Anatomy*, *Scandal*, and *How to Get Away With Murder* – three of the biggest U.S. TV shows of the 21st century.

> **"**
> Not only did my family
> not do a goddamn thing,
> but my dad was also all
> for it. He was the one
> who approved all of it. My
> whole family did nothing.
> **"**

Britney's statement to Judge Brenda Penny, U.S. Court,
regarding her conservatorship, 23 June 2021.

When travelling on tour, Britney invents on-the-spot pseudonyms so hotels cannot alert press to her visit.

Names such as Alotta Warmheart, Anita Dick and Chastity Montgomery have been used, as well as Diana Prince and Abra Cadabra.

> **"**
>
> Good God I love my fans so much it's crazy! I think I'm gonna cry the rest of the day! Best day ever … praise the Lord … can I get an Amen. #FreedBritney.
>
> **"**

Britney, freed from her conservatorship at last, Twitter, 11 December 2021.